Original title:
Heaven by the Sea

Copyright © 2025 Creative Arts Management OÜ
All rights reserved.

Author: Natalia Harrington
ISBN HARDBACK: 978-1-80581-504-4
ISBN PAPERBACK: 978-1-80581-031-5
ISBN EBOOK: 978-1-80581-504-4

Celestial Sanctuary on the Shore

The seagulls chatter like old mates,
With sandwiches plucked from our plates.
A crab moonwalks in his tiny shoes,
Chasing waves while we sip our brews.

The sun wears shades, he's feeling cool,
Building sandcastles, oh what a fool!
We laugh as the tide takes our work away,
"Next time," we shout, "we'll use concrete today!"

Beaches of Whispers and Wonders

The shells are gossiping by the tide,
With secrets only they confide.
Flip-flops slapping, a merry tune,
As we race the waves and leap like a loon.

The sand tickles toes, a gentle tease,
While the sun tan lines offer quite the squeeze.
We toast with shells, our drinks held high,
Laughing at seagulls—did they just fly by?

When the Sky Breathes the Ocean

Clouds stretch like cats in a lazy show,
While kids splash like fish, and time seems slow.
A dolphin flips, with a twist and a splash,
While beach balls zoom by in a wild dash.

Our beach umbrella's a balloon gone astray,
As it dances and flops in a funny ballet.
With laughter echoing under the sun's beams,
We gather sandy memories, woven from dreams.

Luminous Horizons

The sun wears shades, so bright and bold,
While crabs in flip-flops strut, so sold.
Seagulls squawk with a witty decree,
As waves dance around in a playful spree.

Shells gossip secrets in the sand,
Where starfish pose, looking quite grand.
Mermaids laugh as they brush their hair,
Silly seaweed twirls without a care.

Echoes of Aquatic Dreams

Fish trade jokes in bubbles so round,
A dolphin's giggle is the best sound.
Octopuses dab, with their inky art,
Creating masterpieces, a true sea heart.

Seashells wear hats made of wet sand,
While shrimp breakdance in a conga band.
Waves tell tales of treasure and glee,
As starry-eyed turtles sip green tea.

The Pleiades by the Shore

Stars drop in, wearing shades of blue,
Sailboats sway, having fun for two.
Lanterns wink, as they start their chat,
Even the sandpipers wear a hat!

Tide pools bubble with giggles and grins,
Anemones dance, welcoming wins.
Lighthouses blink with cheeky delight,
As sunsets throw a color fight.

Sanctuary of the Almighty

The tides bow low, each wave says 'hi,'
While shrimp in tuxedos dash on by.
A sandcastle holds court, so regal and grand,
While seashell soldiers take their stand.

Starfish debate on the meaning of fate,
With jellyfish hanging out, feeling great.
Seaspray tickles with laughter divine,
As the ocean winks, 'Everything's fine!'

Chasing Light from Wave to Wave

A seagull swoops with grace,
It steals my fries, what a chase!
The sun dips down, a golden gem,
I curse the bird, then laugh at them.

Surfboards dance like silly dogs,
Crabs play tag in sandy bogs,
I tried to surf but fell instead,
The waves just laughed, I'm bruised, but fed.

Ocean's Palette at Dusk

The sky is a painter's great delight,
Twilight whispers, 'not quite night.'
Pinks and purples, a silly show,
I lost my hat—oh where did it go?

Fish swim by in coats of dreams,
While dolphins mimic my silly screams,
I snuggle up with sandy toes,
The ocean giggles, who really knows?

Lost in a Cosmic Drift

A star fell down upon my head,
Swam out far, too far, I said.
Now I float like a jelly fish,
I hope the tide will grant my wish.

Mermaids sing, but I can't dance,
I trip on waves, a clumsy chance,
The moon winks as I flail about,
Oh, life is weird; that's what it's about!

Beneath the Cascading Sky

The clouds roll in, a pillow fight,
I duck and dodge, oh what a sight!
Raindrops chuckle as they splash,
The beach is fun, in a splashy bash.

Kites soar high, they pull my strings,
A seagull dips; it steals my bling!
We laugh together in this sweet storm,
Nature's jokes keep my heart warm.

Reflections in the Brine

A crab wore a hat, quite absurd,
He strutted like a bird, not a word.
Seagulls squawked in a chorus so fine,
As fish rolled their eyes, 'What a sign!'

With sandcastles tall, made for a king,
A toddler declared, 'This is my bling!'
A wave sneezed loudly, knocked it askew,
The toddler just laughed, 'Now that's a new!'

Moonlit Shores and Radiant Skies

Under the moon, a dolphin danced,
Wearing sunglasses, it took a chance.
A starfish, clapping with one little limb,
Said, 'Keep dancing, don't you swim!'

Jellyfish glowed in a disco show,
Flashing lights, they put on a glow.
A crab DJ played, shell-breaking beats,
As clams got cheeky and wiggled their seats.

A Caress of Ocean Breeze

The sea breeze tickled a sailor's hat,
He chased it down, what do you chat?
A fish yelled, 'Buddy, don't lose your flair!'
But the sailor just stumbled, 'Life's not fair!'

With kites in the air, a gull took a dive,
Chasing a sandwich, oh how it thrived!
The beachgoers cheered as it snagged its prize,
While mustard dripped down, oh what a surprise!

Between the Waves and Above the Stars

A starfish dreamt of one day to fly,
With a rocket attached, it aimed for the sky.
The ocean chuckled, 'You're far too flat!'
But the starfish just winked, 'Wait till I chat!'

A whale sang loud, in quirky delight,
'The sky's too cramped; come dance with the night!'
The clouds rolled in, and they all took a spin,
Underneath it all, they wore grins of gin.

Sunlit Waves and Starry Nights

The sun flips pancakes on the waves,
While seagulls dance like silly knaves.
Sandy toes in a giant boot,
Who knew crabs could play the flute?

The stars play peek-a-boo with the tide,
Belly flops from dolphins, they collide.
Shells whisper jokes that float to shore,
A laugh that echoes forevermore.

The Serenity of Salt and Sky

A beach ball war bounces in the breeze,
While jellyfish sip on seaweed teas.
Flip-flops sing songs of summer fun,
As sandcastles sway 'til they're undone.

Chasing waves, a fish wears a cap,
Witty remarks from a drifting map.
Seagulls giggle at the clumsy jog,
While crabs play poker with a sea fog.

Dreaming on the Edge of Paradise

In flip-flops, life's a comic tale,
With every splash, the sea squawks in pale.
Surfers wielding cheesy grins,
Their wipeouts like epic circus spins.

Sunburns paint the skin of the bold,
Like lobster kings in a story told.
A picnic blanket takes off at last,
Sailed away by the wind so fast.

Ocean's Embrace

I found a fish with a bow tie on,
It told me tales of wave-surfing dawn.
Mermaids giggle with ice-cream cones,
While octopuses steal the microphones.

Laughter bubbles up from the shore,
As crabs take selfies, always wanting more.
Under a sun that tickles your nose,
Every tide brings more giggly prose.

The Reckoning of Tides

The tide rolls in with a cheeky grin,
Shells doing a dance, what a silly spin!
Seagulls squawk like they're laughing loud,
As crabs play tag, in their sandy crowd.

With flip-flops flying, a splash in the air,
A kid's ice cream cone? Oh, what a scare!
The ocean's a joker, pulling our toes,
Whispering secrets where the seaweed grows.

An Abode of Dreams and Dunes

In the land of sand where the funny crabs dwell,
The sun plays tricks, casting shadows to tell,
Of sunburned tourists with hats that are wide,
And beach balls bouncing, a colorful ride.

The dunes are soft pillows, oh what a sight,
A gathering place for kites taking flight.
A tumble and roll, whoa, there went my drink!
But laughter erupts; we don't need to think.

Cobalt Reflections

Cobalt waves flicker, a mischievous hue,
A fish with a wink, just swam right on through,
What's that? A flip, oh no, there goes my hat,
The ocean's a prankster, imagine that!

Mirrors of water that tease and surprise,
The seagull brigade all wearing grand ties,
As sunbathers giggle, with sunscreen in hand,
Nature's a stand-up; it's all quite unplanned.

When Waves Sing to the Stars

When the stars show up like a sparkling show,
The waves bust a move, putting on a flow,
With foam-tipped giggles, they leap and they play,
While dolphins pop up for a jolly display.

A beach ball in orbit, a surprising sight,
The moon gives a wink, oh, isn't it bright?
As laughter echoes across the night sky,
The waves sing a tune; oh my, oh my!

Shoreline Seraphim

On the shore they dance and flit,
Wings of seagulls that just won't sit.
Shells are treasures in the sand,
While crabs walk proud, just as they planned.

Mermaids laugh and trade their tales,
While fish wear hats and sail in gales.
But watch the waves; they might just tease,
And tickle toes with salty breeze.

Mysteries of Distant Skies

Clouds like cotton candy float,
A whale's a fish that's learned to gloat.
Stars spill secrets on the tide,
While octopuses play hide and slide.

Look! A comet plays hopscotch bright,
As gulls gossip in fading light.
Aliens sneak snacks from the shore,
While dolphins mix pro surf and lore.

Lighthouses of the Spirit

A lighthouse beams, a watchful eye,
But twice it sneezed—oh my, oh my!
Beacons wink with a quirky shine,
While boats bob and sip on brine.

Shadows dance like silly ghosts,
Giving crabs and clams the most.
With every flash, a chuckle's found,
As surfers ride the waves unbound.

Serene Waters

The waters giggle, softly sway,
In silver pools the fish do play.
A duck with shades floats by with flair,
While turtles grin without a care.

Rippling laughter echoes near,
As seahorses toast with a cheer.
Each bubble pops with a silly sound,
In this place, joy knows no bound.

Starry Night

Stars are sprinkles on the sea,
While crickets sing in harmony.
A moonlit disco starts to spin,
With jellyfish jiving, let's dive in!

The night is young; the cosmos grins,
As shooting stars share goofy wins.
Giggles echo in the sand,
In this vast and wild wonderland.

Journey through Celestial Waters

A fish in a tux, looking quite dapper,
Chasing a bubble, that turned out to be a caper.
Seagulls in shades, they're quite the delight,
Sipping on sodas, under soft moonlight.

Octopus dancing like it's on a spree,
Waves are the rhythm, come join the jamboree!
A crab with a mic starts to croon,
As starfish tap dance to a whimsical tune.

Illuminated Shores

Sandy castles with windows so bright,
Fighting tide monsters in a playful slight.
Beach balls are planets, and shells are the stars,
Sand in our sandwiches—yep, that's ours!

Kites flying high, like fish on a line,
The laughter of gulls forms the sweetest design.
Flip-flops in flight, it's a striking affair,
As we run from the tide, with a splash and a flare.

Radiant Horizons Ahead

Sun like a clown, pops in with a grin,
Bringing the warmth, let the fun begin!
Flip-flopped feet doing the twist by the bay,
Crabs in a conga, oh what a display!

Mermaids trade gossip, they're laughing with glee,
While dolphins do tricks, oh so slyly spree.
Tanned toes and silly hats, is life ever better?
As we dodge the waves, it's light as a feather.

Captured Moments in Aquatic Light

Snorkels and giggles, what a fine sight,
Seashells are treasures hidden from light.
Jellyfish waltzing, soft as a breeze,
Sand dollars gossip, oh, how they tease!

Collecting our splashes, as we laugh and we play,
Waves whisper secrets that fade in the spray.
With each foam hug, our worries take flight,
In the grand aquatic ballet of the night.

Horizon's Promise

The sun's like butter on toast,
Spreading warmth from coast to coast.
Seagulls squawk with much delight,
As they dance in joyful flight.

Sandcastles rise, a grand parade,
Yet the tide's tease can't be delayed.
Down they crash, a sandy flop,
Parents just laugh and never stop.

Elysium's Coast

Flip-flops squeak, a rhythmic tune,
As kids chase waves like a cartoon.
A beach ball flies, a mid-air quest,
Lands on a sunbather's chest.

Umbrella's shade turns from blue to red,
As sunblock's splatters fill my head.
With every splash and goofy smile,
We float and bob, it's worth our while.

Celestial Currents

Shells that whisper secrets dear,
Mermaids giggle, come and hear!
A crab dons shades, struts with flair,
As I trip over my own hair.

Sandy feet lead the way to fun,
While ice cream melts under the sun.
Laughter echoes with every splash,
And kids rocket past in a mad dash.

Tranquil Waters

Surfboards wobble, just like me,
Fish poke fun, as if to see.
A turtle's dive, doing the limbo,
As I flail, oh what a show!

With picnic snacks that crumble fast,
Soda sprays when the lid's unmasked.
Even seagulls cannot resist,
This feast of chaos, quite the list!

Endless Skies

Kites that soar, with colors bright,
Adults act like kids in flight.
A sunburnt nose, a badge of pride,
When laughter waves like a joyful tide.

In this realm where joy abounds,
Every wave brings funny sounds.
While time just drifts and plays around,
We find our bliss on sandy ground.

Waves of Paradise

The ocean swells with laughter loud,
A pelican wearing a snorkel, proud.
Seagulls squawk tunes of birthday songs,
While crabs dance up in their tiny throngs.

Flip-flops fly as kids take their sprint,
Chasing waves with a clumsy hint.
A sandcastle crowned with a soda can,
Under the gaze of a wobbly tan.

Ice cream drips down, sticky and sweet,
Everyone's searching for the next tasty treat.
The tide pulls back with a cheeky flair,
Leaving behind treasures, and someone's hair.

As the sun dips low with a wink and a cheer,
A crab performs stand-up, filling hearts with cheer.
Life's a beach, with jokes on full display,
Let's giggle our way through another sunny day!

The Celestial Coastline

At dusk, the stars gather in a line,
Holding a party, it's quite divine.
Mermaids grinning with glitter and shells,
Offering snacks and tall tales as well.

A dolphin shows off its best silly dance,
While sailors applaud in a water trance.
With flip-flops flying in silly brigade,
The gulls are the judges, unafraid.

The moon wears a hat made of rippling waves,
Laughing at folks who think they're so brave.
Buckets of dreams come chasing ashore,
As beach balls bounce through the laughter galore.

Sandy toes twinkle under night's embrace,
With stars putting on their sparkly lace.
Oh what a show, with fun and delight,
As creatures of water join in the night!

Dreams in Salted Breezes

Salt on our skin, we giggle and play,
Chasing the seagulls that steal our buffet.
Flipped-up chairs in whimsical arcs,
While starfish gossip and share silly remarks.

A beach ball bounces, round and bright,
Crashing onto umbrellas in an awkward flight.
Children burst out with giggles and shrills,
As parents relax, resisting the spills.

Shell collectors swap, bragging as they go,
"Look at my treasure!" "Mine's bigger though!"
Waves crash in rhythm, a comical beat,
As sand swirls high beneath dancing feet.

An octopus juggles out by the rocks,
Causing all passerby to stop and gawk.
With each salty breeze, laughter runs free,
We dance through the chaos, carefree as can be!

Ethereal Reflections

The sunset's glow paints faces aglow,
While a dog steals snacks with a wiggly show.
Neighbors chuckle as the tide rises slow,
Pouring cold water on shoes below.

Laughter erupts from a seashell's tale,
As crabs crinkle jokes without fail.
Each wave whispers secrets with salty delight,
While umbrellas wiggle in a comical flight.

Children race, splashing water with glee,
Till a wave sneaks up, and oh, what a spree!
Laughter erupts like bubbles in air,
While cooler spills, and nobody cares.

Beneath starry skies, the jokes still unfold,
With treasures of laughter worth more than gold.
In the evening breeze, while the moon takes a peek,
A symphony of giggles, all fun, and unique!

Harmonics of the Sea and Sky

The pelicans dance in a line,
With beach balls tossed up high.
Seagulls are crooning their song,
While crabs get up to fly.

Waves roll in with a chuckle,
And tickle the sandy shore.
As dolphins do silly tricks,
They always beg for more.

Sunbathers wear hats too big,
Blocking out the warm sun's rays.
While sunburned and laughing,
They reminisce about their days.

Sandcastles stand proud and tall,
Decorated by seashells bright.
Until a wave laughs too loud,
And gives them quite the fright!

Beyond the Endless Expanse

Far off, the horizon yells,
Promising adventure anew.
But first, let's spill some ice cream,
On that poor seagull's shoe.

Clouds are fluffier than cotton,
Like pillows just tossed a side.
While the sun plays peek-a-boo,
The ocean's got nowhere to hide.

Fishermen tell tall tales,
Of the fish that got away.
But we all know it was just,
Their lunch that stole the day.

Splash fights rage on the shore,
With laughter in every splash.
As sand and water collide,
With no hint of a crash!

Glimmers of Eternity on the Water

The water sparkles like diamonds,
As pirates sing sea shanties.
But the treasure they seek in the sand,
Is just a box of candies.

Bubbles float up to the sky,
Like wishes caught in a net.
While mermaids brush their long hair,
And whisper secrets, you bet!

Footprints dance in the wet sand,
While dolphins play hide and seek.
And everyone stares, mouth agape,
At a clam that begins to speak.

The sun takes its final bow,
Painting the waves with delight.
As night falls, the stars come out,
To giggle at our silly plight.

The Enchantment of the Abyss

Down by the edge of the world,
Octopuses wear bow ties.
While lobsters breakdance around,
It's quite the wild surprise!

Fish in tuxedos waltz,
As the tides keep the rhythm alive.
And jellyfish float by in style,
Buzzing tunes in a jive.

The seaweed sways with laughter,
In the grooves of the ocean floor.
As turtles join in the fun,
And show off some moves galore!

But just when the party peaks,
A whale steals the oceanic scene.
With a loud, cheerful spout,
He reminds us who's the king!

Starlight over Foam

Frogs in tuxedos leap, oh so spry,
They dance on the waves, beneath a twinkling sky.
A crab in a top hat looks quite debonair,
While seagulls are singing, without a single care.

The fish wear sunglasses, swimming with style,
They laugh at old octopuses, who haven't smiled.
Jellyfish in pajamas float past with a grin,
While sea turtles applaud, and the show begins.

Echoes of the Infinite Ocean

The tide whispers secrets with a cheeky laugh,
And starfish trade jokes on the sandy path.
Dolphins wear bowties, leaping in cheer,
As shells provide claps — can you hear?

Crabs debate loudly, who's king of the beach,
While waves throw confetti, within arm's reach.
Rainbow fish gossip, oh what a delight,
In a world made of giggles, beneath the moonlight.

Inspired by the Celestial

A sunflower grew tired of standing so tall,
So it grabbed a surfboard and took a great fall.
With dreams of great heights, it splashed in the blue,
Only to find that its roots liked the view.

Stars with popcorn chat loudly at night,
While waves do the rumba, it's quite a sight!
With each gentle crash, they all share a joke,
As sandcastles shiver and giggle, bespoke.

Sunlit Serenity

Seashells wear hats, sipping lemonade,
While crabs play at poker, their claws unafraid.
Pelicans dive in, hoping for fish,
While seaweed waves hello, granting every wish.

The suncakes are baking, oh what a tease,
Silly sea urchins dance, doing as they please.
With laughter like bubbles, they float through the air,
In a whimsical world, where no one's a care.

Seaside Reverie

The gulls are plotting, or so it seems,
Stealing fries from all our dreams.
Shells are scattered, like lost socks,
Who knew the beach was full of clocks?

A sandcastle stands, a proud domain,
Guarded by crabs that entertain.
Flip-flops dancing with each wave,
A silent battle, but who will save?

Sunburned noses, a sight to behold,
Like tomatoes left in the sun, so bold.
Ice cream drips, a sticky affair,
Chasing seagulls, not a single care!

Endless laughter, the tide rolls in,
We'd swim with dolphins, but can't quite swim.
With every wave a giggle or sigh,
Adventures await, beneath the sky!

Mirage of the Infinite Blue

The ocean looks like a giant pool,
Where fish wear hats and play it cool.
Mermaids surfing on the breeze,
Telling tales that aim to tease.

Seashells gossip, I swear I heard,
Of a crab that dreams of flying birds.
With waves that tickle your painted toes,
And seaweed fashion, who really knows?

Coconuts rolling like wayward balls,
As palm trees dance at summer's calls.
A sunburnt dude tackled by the surf,
Takes laughter to a whole new turf!

The horizon winks with a playful glance,
While starfish join in a jiggly dance.
And seagulls play the air guitar,
Who knew the sea was quite bizarre?

The Dance of Light upon the Sea

The sun is a frisbee, oh so round,
Bouncing rays as it hits the ground.
Waves waltz in sparkly delight,
Dancing shadows, a playful sight.

Jellyfish jiggle in neon glow,
As beach balls go where the currents flow.
Flip-flops flapping, a clumsy beat,
As laughter echoes down the street.

Sandcastles wobble under the sun,
Each tower proudly thinks it's won.
But with each wave, they melt in time,
Ah, the beach—a never-ending rhyme!

So raise your towels and toast the sky,
To sunny days that fizz and fly.
With every giggle, a joyous spree,
Happiness found by the playful sea!

Where the Sky Kisses the Water

Sky and water share a messy kiss,
To waves that murmur, well, what's amiss?
Clouds in flip-flops hover about,
While fish tease each other without a doubt.

A kite gets tangled in a seagull's hair,
An artistic feat, but who would dare?
With sunscreens flying every which way,
We squirt the kids and laugh at play.

The horizon's giggle, a soft embrace,
As jellybeans try to win a race.
Sandy faces, with chocolate stains,
Tickle fights rolling through sunny lanes.

So here we sit, in joyful retreat,
With shells as trophies, it's hard to beat!
In this land of whimsy and salty cheer,
Life's a beach, and the vibe's quite clear!

Illumined Waves of Tranquility

Bubbles dance with glee, afloat,
While seagulls squawk like they're on a boat.
A crab in shades, it struts with flair,
All the while, fish ponder if we care.

Sandcastles rise, then meet their doom,
A wave comes crashing, a watery tomb.
Children squeal, run, and then fall flat,
Nature's prankster, where're your stats?

Sunset paints the sky with gold,
Barefoot joggers trying to be bold.
In flip-flops lost, they stumble and trip,
While ice cream drips, oh what a slip!

Laughter echoes, the day slips away,
As beach balls bounce, come what may.
Joy swims in every corner so bright,
In this watery realm, all feels just right.

The Divine Tide

Waves roll in with a cheerful song,
They tease the shore where they belong.
Umbrella hats bobble, bright and fun,
Guess who forgot to put on sunscreen, hon?

Starfish stars, they strike a pose,
While sand dollars whisper, 'when do we close?'
Crab races commenced, a shell-shaped track,
Flip-flops clashing—hey, watch your back!

Seashell bands play a tune so sweet,
With jellyfish dancing on their feet.
Seagulls overhead, they shout with glee,
One stole my sandwich—how rude is he?

As day turns dusk, the sky on fire,
We toast with soda, what a delight!
In this cheerful realm, let laughter ring,
Where every splash feels like a fling.

Whispers of the Tides

A sandy tummy rub, the tide whispers low,
While beachgoers play, on they go!
Buckets filled with dreams and sand,
Where mermaids giggle on their land.

Sunscreen battles li'l ones fight,
A sticky mess, oh, what a sight!
Kites take flight with a breeze that's fine,
While folks applaud, 'Look, it's all mine!'

Waves clapping, a standing ovation,
As the catch of the day brings commotion.
Fishing rods bend, "Oh what a thrill!"
Not just for fish, but for lunch as a meal.

Under the shade, with drinks we cheer,
As crabs do the moonwalk, oh dear!
With beachy tunes and laughter so sweet,
In this amusing sandcastle retreat.

Celestial Shores

The sun dips low with a wink so sly,
As twilight toes dip into the sky.
A whale of a joke bounces off the waves,
While dolphins gossip, 'Oh, how it behaves!'

Lighthouses flash their disco lights,
Guiding lost pelicans on wild flights.
Sand dollars play poker, that's no bluff,
It's a tough game if your luck's not enough!

Surfboards dance like they've lost their minds,
As tourists tumble in hilariously missed finds.
The foam carries whispers of secrets untold,
Of shovels and snack packs, that grand heist bold.

As stars twinkle like jellybeans in the sky,
We laugh and share stories as time flits by.
With gentle waves weaving tales that please,
We find our joy amid the salty breeze.

Enchanted Shores

Seagulls giggle in the breeze,
Crabs dance like they're on the keys.
Sandcastles lean, they wave goodbye,
As waves come crashing, oh my, oh my!

Beach balls bounce with a silly cheer,
While sunscreen's splattered, what a smear!
Flip-flops fly, then land like a clown,
Running from seagulls, oh, what a frown!

Shells pretend to sing a tune,
While kids chase jellyfish under the moon.
The tides pull laughter, waves pull sighs,
Not a dull moment beneath the skies!

A picnic blanket, pizza galore,
Seagulls plotting for a slice or four.
As sunset colors begin to blend,
The beach is a comedy that never ends!

Tranquility Beyond the Horizon

Waves whisper secrets, oh so light,
While surfers tumble in comedic flight.
Napping dolphins plot their next prank,
As fishermen's boats sink, let's be frank!

Beach towels spread like giant pizzas,
While sunscreen battles against the breezes.
Flip-flops slapping makes a merry tune,
As crabs act like they own the dune!

Children build towers that wobble and sway,
The kingdom of sand, hip-hip-hooray!
Seagulls steal chips while everyone gasps,
Just another day of funny mishaps!

The sun dips low, still laughing bright,
As night brings stars that twinkle just right.
With belly laughs echoing in the night,
What a delightful, comical sight!

Harmonies of Sky and Sea

The ocean sings a silly song,
As waves splash back, 'You've been wrong!'
Seagulls strut in their best attire,
While beachcombers search for treasure to hire!

Kites do battle with stadium fans,
While sunburned kids play expert dance.
A crab in a hat steals the show,
Waving his claws as he moves to and fro!

Sandcastles crumble, but who needs a throne?
With friends beside you, you're never alone.
The beach becomes a circus of joy,
With laughter and silliness, oh what a ploy!

As twilight wraps its arms so wide,
We gather 'round the fire with pride.
Stories of blunders and mishaps galore,
Are what make this beach so hard to ignore!

Embracing the Infinite Blue

Under the sun, a goofy parade,
Where flip-flops fly and pranks are laid.
Paddleboards wobble with comedic flair,
As sunbathers nap, unaware of the air!

Waves like jesters dance and tease,
While children bubble over with glee.
A giant inflatable starts to deflate,
As laughter bubbles, it's never too late!

Bonfire tales grow taller each year,
With marshmallows flying—oh dear, oh dear!
While shadows do a silly jig,
As stars come out, let's have a big gig!

As night wraps around with twinkling eyes,
The beach hums laughter under the skies.
With friends and folly, we revel and cheer,
In this dreamy spot, year after year!

Zephyr's Breath over Crystal Waves

In sandals worn and sunblock smeared,
We danced like fish, oh how we cheered!
With every splash, the seagulls shriek,
Flipping fries was our favorite tweak.

A crab in shades, he sang a tune,
While dolphins laughed and chased the moon.
Our beach ball soared, then whacked a mat,
'Twas just warm sand, we hardly spat.

The waves were high, the laughter loud,
While locals stared, brightly proud.
We built a castle, armada steep,
But only crabs would dare to keep.

Yet in this realm of sand and jest,
We found our joy, we found our rest.
With playful wishes and salty air,
Our giggles danced on seaside flair.

A Horizon of Dreams

With dreams afloat on a jellyfish,
We surfed the breeze, a salty wish.
Our sun hats spun in wild delight,
As sandcastles crumbled, what a sight!

The seagulls cawed, all filled with glee,
Stealing chips from folks like me.
A clam with style, in one shoe only,
Critiqued our moves, oh so homely!

The skies turned pink as we made plans,
To open shops selling sand in cans.
We'd sell two shells, a starfish, too,
With sticky notes, to say we're "you"!

As waves applauded our silly dreams,
We tossed our cares like beach ball seams.
From dawn till dusk, we laughed and played,
In this grand place where fun won't fade.

Starlight Pathways

Underneath the twinkling lights,
We searched for stars, oh what delights!
The piña coladas swayed in hand,
As we sought truths in the shifting sand.

A turtle danced a lovely jig,
While flames flickered, bright and big.
We joined him too, albeit quite slow,
With not a care which way to go!

The comets laughed, we took our stance,
Attempted to have our own moon dance.
But tripping over flip-flops once more,
We rolled like waves, and laughed on the shore.

In this faint glow, where dreams collide,
We spun our tales and cast aside.
In giggling whispers, we all would sway,
Until the stars blinked, and stole away.

Where the Ocean Meets the Cosmos

With cosmic sands that tickle toes,
We divine the ocean's funny prose.
Each wave a joke that lands just right,
A belly flop? Oh what a sight!

The ocean hums, a silly tune,
While crabs attempt a trumpet's croon.
We sought out aliens, just for fun,
But found a beach ball, our lunar sun.

Paddle boards sailed with alien dreams,
"Take me to your leader," one of them beams.
As starfish danced like they'd won a prize,
We joined their groove, 'neath starlit skies.

With laughter rolling in tidal waves,
We found our peace in the jest of braves.
For where we play, a universe plays,
In giggles and waves, we spent our days.

Embraced by the Infinite

Waves laugh like children, playing so bright,
Seagulls tell secrets, take wing in flight.
Shells wear their hats, a quirky parade,
While crabs strut their stuff, unafraid.

Flip-flops are dancing on golden sand,
I trip over one, now I'm in a band!
Coconuts wink, they're full of good cheer,
As I try to juggle, my skills aren't clear.

Sunscreen-smeared faces, a sight to behold,
An octopus chuckles, or so I am told.
Sunset paints skits with colors so bright,
As we laugh 'til we cry, well into the night.

With toes in the water, I might just stay,
Though the tide's pulling me, it's won't have its way.
Life's a beach, and I'm ready to play,
Who knew fun could come in such a salty bouquet?

Horizon's Lullaby

The ocean hums softly, a ticklish tune,
I try to join in, but sound like a loon.
Fish flip their tails, they're the real rock stars,
My chair's drifting away, I'm sailing to Mars.

Sandcastles tumble, they laugh as they fall,
My bucket's a sieve, it won't hold at all.
Seashells are giggling, they're in on the joke,
As I slip on a jellyfish, oh boy, what a poke!

Waves come a-bouncing, they're playful and spry,
While I'm wrestling seaweed that tries to fly by.
With each little splash, I hear ocean's delight,
Who knew the shoreline could feel so light?

As nightfall approaches, with twinkling stars,
The moon joins our party, that funny old czar.
We pop some sea popcorn, oh what a surprise,
In this ocean of laughter, the fun never dies!

The Divine Coast

On sandy runways, the crabs hold their race,
I'm the announcing snail, keeping a pace.
Seaweed's the flag, that sways left and right,
As clams cheer them on with all of their might.

Dolphins are diving, with flips in the air,
But my belly flop steals all the attention, I swear!
With laughter like waves crashing down on the shore,
Who needs a trophy when you can have more?

Pineapples giggle, they're wearing sun hats,
While fish share the stage with these quirky spats.
The tide's pulling tricks, it swaps left and right,
Bringing back treasures from morning till night.

As the sun bows out, the sky starts to glow,
The ocean whispers tales that only we know.
Grab your silly hats, let's dance in the foam,
With giggles and splashes, the coast feels like home!

Solace at Water's Edge

On the water's edge, we've made quite a scene,
With sand in our hair, it's a glamorous sheen.
A floaty mishap sends my hat soaring high,
As a pelican swoops, it gives me the eye.

Kites are in tangles, a colorful mess,
Seagulls are laughing, it's anyone's guess.
Shells hum along with a whimsical beat,
While I trip on a flip-flop – oh, what a feat!

Bubbles are popping, like laughter set free,
I chase them around like they're fish in the sea.
The sun's wearing shades, it's taking a break,
While clouds throw confetti, for fun's sake!

As twilight unfolds, with colors so grand,
We gather together, a whimsical band.
With tales of our day, we chuckle with glee,
At this shore full of joy — just you and me!

Serenity of Starlit Shores

The moon fell into a cup of tea,
While seagulls danced with glee.
Crabs wear hats with flair,
Oh, what a sight right there!

Waves whisper jokes in the breeze,
Shells giggle as they tease.
The fish in tuxedos swim,
Having fun on a whim!

Starfish play cards on the sand,
While the tide makes its stand.
Each wave a laugh, a cheer,
What a party every year!

So bring your snack and a chair,
The seaside welcomes all who dare.
With laughter rising like the tide,
In this silly seaside ride!

Celestial Dancers of the Sea

The waves waltz under starlit beams,
Fish wear shoes, or so it seems.
Turtles in tutus twirl around,
While the deep bass thumps the ground.

Seashells gossip through the night,
As jellyfish glow in delight.
The tides tickle the sandy feet,
This ocean party can't be beat!

Crabby conga lines parade,
In the moonlight, they've got it made.
Starfish snap their claws to the beat,
Dance till dawn, oh what a treat!

So join the fun, bring your flair,
Where laughter mingles with the air.
The sea's a stage, the stars our song,
In this merry world, we all belong!

Drifting through a Sea of Stars

Drifting by in a boat of dreams,
Catching fish that fill the seams.
The stars like sprinkles on the cake,
Even dolphins laugh and shake!

Sneaky seagulls steal our fries,
While sandcastles rise to the skies.
A crab a-laughing as he eats,
Singing loud to the rhythmic beats!

Drifting clouds, a playful sight,
While the sun takes a nap at night.
The boat is rocked by a playful whale,
Telling tales of a great fish tale!

Laughter echoes through the waves,
As we dance with splashy braves.
The sea and stars unite, you see,
In this wacky jubilee!

Sands of Time and Stars

On sands that tickle toes so sweet,
Time does a jig, skipping on its feet.
With each grain, a giggle hid,
As crabs recite jokes that they did!

Waves run up to play peekaboo,
Tickling shells, 'How do you do?'
The stars above clap their hands,
Joining in on this fun with bands!

Seashells laugh as they tell their lore,
Of mermaids who dance on the ocean floor.
A starfish spins like a ballerina,
While the tides play scenes from a patina!

So gather round, it's a starry spree,
With dancing waves and a splash of glee.
The universe smiles, we're part of the show,
In this joyful carnival, we all glow!

Whispers of the Tides

The seagulls squawk with glee,
A crab's lost its cup of tea.
Waves dance like a silly clown,
As dolphins wear their best frown.

Shells giggle under the sun,
Whispers of tides have begun.
Starfish stuck on a beach chair,
Shout out loud, 'It's not fair!'

Sandy toes play peek-a-boo,
While the fish wrestle by the blue.
Barnacles chant a sea shanty,
And jellyfish move like they're fancy.

In the breeze, the seaweed sways,
Telling tales of silly days.
A mermaid's hair in a twist,
Says, 'Oh, what a day to exist!'

Celestial Shores

On the shore where the sand's a treat,
A clam has lost its favorite seat.
The tide pulls in with a goofy grin,
While barnacles try to spin and spin.

Clouds drift by like fluffy sheep,
While the ocean waves make a leap.
A fish in a tie orders ice cream,
In this sandy place, what a dream!

A crab tries to dance, but oh what a flop,
The waves laugh as they bubble and pop.
Seagulls argue over a French fry,
While a whispering breeze floats on by.

Beneath a sun with a silly face,
Everyone wears their bathing grace.
With laughter and splashes that never cease,
They enjoy their absurd ocean piece.

Above the Ocean's Embrace

Kites flying high with a squeal,
Fish wearing hats like it's no big deal.
The sun winks down with a playful spin,
While beach balls bounce, let's begin!

A pufferfish dances with flair,
As seagulls pirouette in the air.
The tide pulls back, playing peek-a-boo,
With crabs that chase their own shadow too.

Shells gossip on the sandy floor,
While waves tell jokes, always wanting more.
A tired dolphin yawns with a grin,
Thinking, 'Oh, why must I always swim?'

In this wild place where laughter abounds,
Life is a game with silly sounds.
Bubbles pop like confetti in flight,
In this whimsical splash of delight!

Celestial Horizons

A beach ball bounces like a star,
Sandy feet dance both near and far.
The sun's a jester, bright and bold,
Sharing secrets that never grow old.

Seashells laugh as they tell a tale,
Of a fish who tried to ride a whale.
The tide rolls in, pulling at shoes,
Bringing back whispers of silly news.

A starfish plays a ukulele tune,
As seagulls swoon under the moon.
The ocean twirls with bubbly cheer,
While the sand whispers, 'We're all here!'

A hermit crab tries on a shoe,
Declaring, 'This fits, what about you?'
With laughter and waves all around,
This jolly beach is truly renowned!

Tidebooks and Dreamscapes

Waves laugh and dance in sunlit glee,
A seagull quips, 'This is the place to be!'
Sandcastles rise, but they always fall,
    Just like my diet—ignore it all!

Crabs throw parties, dressed fine in shells,
They pinch my toes and ring their bells.
  A beach ball rolls, it starts to flee,
  Whose idea was it to invite a bee?

  Sunburned nose, but spirits are high,
Sipping juice beneath the bright blue sky.
My shades are ridiculous, but I don't care,
I'm too busy daydreaming, floating in air!

So here's to laughter, to fun and to play,
  Chasing the tide, come join the fray!
  With sandy toes and salt-kissed skin,
We dance to the rhythm—let the fun begin!

Ascending with the Winds

Kites tangled in laughter, soaring so high,
While the wind whispers secrets, it's hard to deny.
The beachcomber stumbles, trips on a shell,
I can't stop laughing; it's funny as hell!

Balloons float by like dreams in the air,
Giggling children spin, without a care.
A seagull swoops in, I shout, 'Hey, no thanks!'
He steals my fries—it's gone in the ranks!

I chase after waves, they're slippery fun,
While my friend mumbles, 'Can we just run?'
Sand in my sandwich, sticky and bright,
But laughter spills out—it feels just right!

So we'll keep playing till the day fades away,
In this joyful realm where we bask and sway.
With grins wide as the sea, let's dive headfirst,
In a world of delight, where giggles burst!

Star-Crossed by the Waters

Two starfish meet, in a twist of fate,
'You're too salty!' one says, 'It's too late!'
They roll their eyes, but can't break apart,
Who knew love would come sea-salt from the heart?

A boat drifts by, with laughter and cheer,
But the captain spills punch, the crew disappears!
Paddles turn to sinkers, they're flailing about,
While I just grin—it's what fun's about!

Fins flapping wildly, a fish makes a scene,
Twirling around like a little marine queen.
'Catch me if you can!' it bubbles with flair,
But even a dolphin can't swim without care!

As sunsets paint skies in shades of delight,
We'll toast to the sea, a star-studded night.
With giggles and waves, let's frolic and dance,
In our own little world, each moment's a chance!

In the Arms of the Endless Blue

Flippers and flip-flops make the best pair,
Splashing through puddles without a care.
A dolphin's doing tricks, oh what a feat!
While I'm still stuck on these sandy feet!

Picnics of sandwiches dancing with ants,
I asked for a quiet day, but just get prance!
The tide comes in, but I'm stuck on the shore,
Is it too much to ask for less ocean and more?

Umbrellas fly past like they've lost their minds,
Chasing the seagulls, what hilarity finds!
With laughter that echoes, we've got it made,
In this silly scene where enjoyment won't fade!

So bring on the waves, the laughs, and the cheer,
With friends by my side, there's nothing to fear.
In the arms of this chaos, I've found my perfect way,
To dance through this journey—come laugh, come play!

Melodies from the Water's Edge

Seagulls squawk in perfect tune,
As beach balls bounce beneath the moon.
A crab in shades, oh what a sight!
Chasing flip-flops with all its might.

The waves clap hands, they have a show,
While I sip lemonade, nice and slow.
A dolphin dances, a funny leap,
In my sand castle, a furry sheep.

Sandy toes wiggle, feeling grand,
A starfish waves, it's on the stand.
The surfboard's stuck in a patch of sea,
Oh, why won't it sail, it's just like me!

With laughter echoing all around,
Each splash and giggle, pure joy is found.
As the tide rolls in, what a sight to see,
Making memories with a splash of glee.

Embracing the Salted Air

Salty breezes tickle my nose,
As I trip over my sun hat's woes.
A pelican swoops, what a clumsy flight,
He misses the fish and lands with a fright!

Jellyfish jokes I tell with flair,
While building a fortress without a care.
A seagull steals my sandwich away,
I guess he likes tuna on a sunny day!

Children's laughter fills the warm sky,
As I fumble through shell games, oh my!
A wave crashes, taking me down,
I rise all soggy, but never a frown.

The sun dips low, painting skies bright,
With giggles and splashes, life feels just right.
Salted air wraps us all in delight,
Funny moments that spark pure light.

Glimmers of Dawn on the Coast

Dawn breaks, and the beach wakes with cheer,
A crab in pajamas crawls near.
Sandcastles topple with each new tide,
While I chase my coffee, what a ride!

Seashells giggle in shades of pink,
Waves whisper secrets, making me think.
As seagulls compete for the best fish meal,
One takes a tumble - oh, what a steal!

The sun shines bright, pretending to prance,
While kids in the waves attempt a dance.
A funny old dog steals someone's hat,
With a wag of its tail, that sneaky brat!

As the morning unfolds, we laugh and play,
Each moment a treasure in sandy ballet.
With glimmers of joy sprouting for free,
Life here is funny, like a wild spree.

The Lure of Shoreline Serenity

A pelican's dive captures my gaze,
But misses its mark, oh what a phase!
The sun shines bright, splashing sparkles wide,
As I trip over driftwood, a silly ride.

Shells scattered like candy on the shore,
As the tide's laughter rolls in with a roar.
I challenge a crab to a race today,
I lose, of course, but it's all a play!

Laughter erupts when a wave grows bold,
Soaks my towel and turns me to gold.
Footprints trailing like a silly parade,
We follow the silliness, never dismayed.

With each splash and giggle, the day marches on,
Under a sky where worries are gone.
The allure of joy in the air is so free,
Bringing smiles and laughter, like a warm cup of tea.

Elysium Beneath the Waves

When fish wear hats and dance on sand,
Starfish high-fives, it's quite unplanned.
Jellybeans float, so bright and round,
In a world where giggles always abound.

Crabs in tuxedos, what a sight!
They waltz by the moon, under starlight.
Seashells whisper jokes of the day,
Telling tales in a silly way.

Octopuses juggling with glee,
Swimming in circles, just like me!
Seaweed sways with a funky beat,
Join the conga, it's a hoot, so sweet!

Bubbles chuckle, float to the sky,
With every pop, they burst and fly.
Turtles hold parties, it's quite bizarre,
Underwater fun, it's a sea-star!

The Blissful Expanse

In the depths where the giggles glow,
Mermaids are trading canoe for a row.
Dolphins wear shades, looking so cool,
Splashing about, an aquatic school.

Seahorses acting like they're the boss,
They strut and they flail, they never gloss.
With each burst of laughter, they ripple and sway,
Making waves that dance, what a fun ballet!

Beach balls float, the sun beams wide,
Sandy feet twirl, sharing smiles side by side.
A clam's great joke brings all to cheer,
While starfish play cards, with a pint of beer!

The tides, they giggle, they tickle the shore,
As seagulls crack wise, wanting to score.
Life's a big party where laughter prevails,
In this ocean of joy, all our hearts sail!

Tranquil Blue Reveries

The sun dips low in a splashy haze,
Fish with party hats, swimming in a daze.
Sharks in tuxes, a formal affair,
Ballet on waves, what a splendid scare!

Octopus pirates share their loot,
Counting their jewels, wearing a boot.
Starfish grinning, they crowd the scene,
With jellybeans bouncing, it's quite the dream.

Corals chuckle, wearing crowns of foam,
As the sea cucumbers find a new home.
The crabs do the twist while fish keep it light,
With a splash of mayonnaise, what a delicious sight!

Mollusks are laughing, they join the parade,
Making waves of joy, a tangy charade.
Underwater art, it's a sight to see,
Where every creature is wild and free!

Celestial Currents

In waters where chuckles bounce and gleam,
The clams spin tales of a quirky theme.
Nautilus playing hide and seek,
Among coral gardens, laughter's peak.

The waves invite all to take a dive,
With sea otters splashing, they truly thrive.
Bubble parties swell, float high above,
From a goofy dolphin, it's joy, not love.

Squids in a tug-of-war with their ink,
Puppets of mirth in briny pink.
A party of flippers, fins oh so bright,
Under the stars, what a magical night!

The tide brings giggles, the moon gives a grin,
As seashells serenade each frolicking fin.
Among ripples and bubbles, the spirit will soar,
In the splash of delight, who could ask for more?

www.ingramcontent.com/pod-product-compliance
Lightning Source LLC
Chambersburg PA
CBHW072222070526
44585CB00015B/1453